T0129904

Philosophy
Management

Philosophy Management

Developing a Philosophy for Managment

FEMI OBASUN

authorHOUSE®

AuthorHouse™
1663 Liberty Drive
Bloomington, IN 47403
www.authorhouse.com
Phone: 1 (800) 839-8640

© 2015 Femi Obasun. All rights reserved.

No part of this book may be reproduced, stored in a retrieval system, or transmitted by any means without the written permission of the author.

Published by AuthorHouse   11/10/2015

ISBN: 978-1-5049-6016-8 (sc)
ISBN: 978-1-5049-6017-5 (e)

Library of Congress Control Number: 2015918570

Print information available on the last page.

Any people depicted in stock imagery provided by Thinkstock are models, and such images are being used for illustrative purposes only.
Certain stock imagery © Thinkstock.

This book is printed on acid-free paper.

Because of the dynamic nature of the Internet, any web addresses or links contained in this book may have changed since publication and may no longer be valid. The views expressed in this work are solely those of the author and do not necessarily reflect the views of the publisher, and the publisher hereby disclaims any responsibility for them.

Contents

Leadership Philosophy Mapping.. vii

Introduction.. xi

My First Business Venture 1

Philosophy of Leadership... 7

Communication Other Key Elements of Structure.......... 13

Organizational Structure.. 17

Environmental Issues... 23

The Core Elements... 27

Conceptual Transformation 31

Conclusion 33

References 37

Leadership Philosophy Mapping

CHAPTER OUTLINE

Leadership

Definition of management philosophy Leadership

Need for Leadership

Patterns of Organizational

Leadership Traits

My First Business framework for managing Search of Leadership

Self-confident

Physical Traits story

Confidence

Personality Traits

Philosophy Leadership

Feed your leadership speculation, values, principle

Leadership

Change naturally

Principles and values for leaders, feed your leadership speculation

Communication other key elements of structure

Top Down, Democratic, an

Initiating Structure and Consideration

Production-centered and Employee -

Centered--Circulation

Leader Behaviors- decoding workers

Managerial Grids- structure cognizant

Situational Leadership

Organizational structure

Managerial Grids hierarchies

Leadership

Path-Goal Model

Normative Decision-Making Model of Leadership

Environmental issues

Humanize myself in humility

Choosing a Leadership Style

Strategies for Improvement

In-house activity and outer environments

Core Element

Proprietorship, S or C Corporation, LLC, or Limited

Conceptual Transformation

Creatively about, analyze and understand complicated and abstract ideas

Developing a Philosophy of management principles, values, styles, etc.

Introduction

A management philosophy is one of the ways we perceive leaders. This book will illustrate my experience in business management style for the past 20 years as a CEO, President, of Obasun Com, GTE, Cellular one, WolrdCom, (MCI). Our practices, as well as principles, including external events shape our philosophy. Leadership learns to change naturally over time by changing our philosophy of management during the current time. In this book, I will show the principles of my core philosophies of management over the past 20 years.

Formulating our leadership philosophy means that you must search plus follow superimposed individual values, presuppositions and, including ideas about leadership. That was very important to me in opening my first business at age of eighteen and a half, but was easy for me because of my family values. I came from the parents of business owners and educators for over 35 years. Your values dictate your purposes and management style. When individual values remain transparent, you are mindful of them, and then it builds a solid framework for managing.

My First Business Venture

At the beginning of my first business GTE Wireless, it was hard fostering a concept or business plan. It was also a confusing time in my life. Confusing because two years earlier in 1994, I finished dead last in my high school ranking in grade point average. Also, had many Athletic Scholarship Offers, had offers and call in 1993 from Coach Frank Beamer currently the head football coach at Virginia Tech. As a shy boy, I didn't handle the call very well. Coach Beamer Said, "I want you to come to Virginia Teach and play for us Femi, but your Grade is bad, So I can get you into the school, but you be redshirted. Plus set out a year or two, since your SAT scores are low." I was nervous also gave a wrong answer. I said, "No, I don't Seat out to nothing." I hanged up the phone before he can even say goodbye. I walked away in the middle of the hallway and ran into my dad. He said, "What happened?" Now, it hard to remember the exact word, but it was in the lines of "no or he want me to seat out." At this point in life, I was very shy but high on self-confident, but very stupid rejecting two or more other scholarships football offers. I can now seat back and reasons why those actions took place. Remember at the beginning of my introduction I reflected on both my parents being educators. One is a PhD. in business, the other a Master in Management. Imagine what I heard every day while in school, it wasn't your great Football player, wrestler or track runner. It was get your grades up and become a doctor or lawyer. Superimpose individual value is the main core of my value that was imposed by my parents.

After graduation, which I did not attend, since again, "I don't seat out to nothing." You know, that self-confident I talked about, not taking the back seat or last place. About two months before graduating I in role in a Community College, and completed a two-year degree in six months, with AA degree, and a grade point average of 3.6. At this point in my life, my high leadership style was changing from highs self-confident to moderate learning self-confident.

In the summer of 1995, I accepted a scholarship to the Virginia Military Institution for Wrestling from the only Coach, who didn't' call me or try to visit. I accepted because he was the only coach that sent a letter instead of a phone call. After one and a half year at VMI, I transferred out. After realizing two factors, one being I lost 65 colleges credit to start over as freshmen. As freshmen wrestler, I was rank number three in the nation plus my second year one or two ranking in the nation. I realized that was only there for wrestling. Plus my grades were low; I was injured too by the Heavyweight Wrestler in a drill, in front of the coach. The coach neglect to discipline the jealous wrestler who had never beaten me in a one and one match.

In the of fall 1997, I was attending George Mason University needing 15 to 20 credit to finish my bachelor. At a time in my life some principal value I retained now are from then, including the value my parent implant in me became the reflection my life today. I went on transferring out of GMU, to finish my bachelors and masters elsewhere. The same time I attended school in 1997 I also started, which help me develop my philosophy style of management over the years.

Philosophy of Leadership

Philosophy leadership is based on principles and values for leaders, is essential to understand what presumptions feed your leadership speculation. For me, it was the core value, the reflection of my parents. More frequently leaders are not knowledgeable of their speculation, their wants, or what they born to do. That is because there acting individual criteria that will not allow them to see speculation. Their reflection on an individual leadership is an invaluable way to reveal their speculation.

My speculation came about in fall 1997, taking my small investment of $15,000 to open first franchise store. After, three months in business we were a ready to close doors with mounting debts of $35,000.00. Leadership has to do what your belief system is. Beliefs are ideas that we carry to be valid; they fashion one mind, including each certainty. Reflecting on my idea of effective management at that point, I dug down on what I believe is one of the best methods to building a successful business. I acknowledge that my management method has modified by putting the focus on retainer leadership (parents), changing my individual management style and continue to endeavor. Circumstances did change in the fourth month when that belief system talked about earlier kicked in gear. The fourth-month gross went from a 0-average to $50,000 a month, this was because of my next topic Organization structure.

There has to be a need to redefine specific components or maybe adopt new methods that will enhance management leadership style. Structure Core is important that is the ethos or the components that brand your company (Nagy., n.d.). Upon hiring a manager we branded new components of marketing. Introduced telemarketing plus marketing dialing system which in all gave us a first-year gross of $170,000, to a fourth year gross of $1,000,000.00. One store front to four different storefronts, plus two mall location. Organizational arrangement determines the functions of management including for all other workers.

Distressed companies are meant to fail. Mostly occurs when the design and structure create uncertainty within a company. In my case, we grew too fast and had a lack of organization between managers. Incompetent workers, were not partaking concepts of the company, plus delayed in decision-making that produce manager's additional problems, pressure, and dispute. The author top of the establishment of each corporation are unconscious to these enigmas or, wrong, move them off as difficulties to surmount or possibilities to advance another. In my particular experience, we move the problems to the next enigmas. Eventually in 2005 our doors close due to poor decision making and management roles. Ending a nine businesses do to (MCI) WorldCom Wireless declare bankruptcy. Till today MCI still owe us as a company $86,000 in commission $250,000 residual revenue, that was forgiven in the bankruptcy.

There are various core elements of organizational structure on three components that are essential in the very idea of organizational construction:

1. Governance: an individual fundamental component of the structure is governance for an organization making the decisions within the business.

2. Organization rules of operation: Rules precisely main division of labor.

3. Work distribution: signs, etc. For example, no noise sign, stop sign.

The assumption of a leader in an organization is to be the father figure, the provider. To assume individuals wants, to make the decisions for the staff, and then that belief system.

Communication Other Key Elements of Structure

The connection of command that circles all workers and the uninterrupted chain of command. The conversation technique is how messages circulate throughout a business. Communication can run from the top down to the bottom. A down through the regiment of management system such communication should proceed horizontally between staff or working group. Formalization illustrates show a regularity systems, for decision-making, plus communication, including management controller. Decision-making is each primary core decision-making jurisdiction at the top of the company focus. All focus on decoding the decision-making pushing down to lower corporation planes.

The spread of communication direction is another component in a corporation composition that relates to the representation of workers that report to a supervisor. An establishment with a high formation has more strong planes including a small span of problems. In distinction, a level formation company has a greater span of power also limited, hierarchal levels. Perpendicular differentiation designates the totality of hierarchal planes within the top directors and workers.

Division level of directors of organization methods is the formulation of the firm's composition. A organization's composition commences the symmetrical responsibilities that are allocated to agencies and persons. It also explains the formal reporting connections including the chain of command, the representation of hierarchical planes, decision makers, plus the directors in control; and guarantees coordination with workers transversely in all the departments. Perpendicular control of a business is implemented within a set of precise tasks including balanced relationships. A visible control is also needed for a perpendicular control to be founded in a firm's organizational chart.

Organizational Structure

Companies vary in capacity also scope, plus a corporate structure should stand developed to satisfy the needs of each worker. Both in-house including outer environmental determinants can end any businesses. The organizational composition is partially influenced by the outer environment, plus companies that stand form to the function within a steady environment may not hold sufficient in a swiftly developing environment. Particularly we know a company with centralized hierarchy is sufficient though companies with an extraordinary level of question are less experienced with decision-making and fewer hierarchies.

In existence are multiple examples of organizational structure. Utmost businesses are created to develop to embrace components of both hierarchies plus more adjustable basic structures within the companies. These below are some models of organizational structures:

The example shows Advantages including Disadvantage.

1. Practical Structure: Advantage, unique departmental purposes and distinct, Example, estimating department, a human resources department, plus the stock department. Individually, each is led by an administrator that reports to the owner. Companies with useful formations have an edge of the experience to be productive when useful jobs are of surpassing value.

   The disadvantage is that the operative objective may be clouded. The overall purposes of the business are a purpose driving department. The author Grimley relates to the composition of an establishment department existence based on the parties of each performing the organization service including is advantageous for enhancing productivity plus experience.

2. Class structure: Disadvantage regulated by Directors or consumer position. The respective division is

nonpartisan plus has a class administrator who reports to the owner.

Advantages respective department is open to channel its production moreover the consequences fall on whom? That becomes a disadvantage application may be reproduced over and over completing the same task.

3. Simplistic structure: Advantage is used in a small setting company level. Representatives normally in teams with whoever is communicating to one leader. The advantages are that it is adaptable plus liabilities are clear.

   Disadvantage is when barrier occurs then your force to deal with that one owner

4. Model Step structure or Matrix: The advantage is that the company will concentrate on divisional production

at a similar period. They are also administering function together plus share all their resources.

The disadvantage is the difficulty of the two hierarchies including the pressures within the two.

5. Network structure: The main focus of the operation is a diplomatic action for the business. Although, subcontracting this operating cost is an advantage, such form of structure is lucrative.

The disadvantage is imminent failure, helplessness depending on other parties, enduring the problem of those subcontractors.

Before starting my businesses it was not ideal for me structurally to create a structure cognizant of the aforementioned factors.

Environmental Issues

Environmental concerns are essential to recognize the influence that the in-house activity and outer environments place on a company structure. The outer environment influence all companies also incorporates matters as, tax, audit, the law, plus political establishment. The in-house work environment likewise has an impact on structural design including concerns for day-to-day transactions, such as adequate operation capital. Technology requirement must also be observed when starting a business. Company's structure varies within the technologies that are needed; this is based on size or complexity of the company.

What structural design requirement is needed for a good reporting business? Well, the environment required technology, however, many other factors, cash flow, customer base, and marketing. The scope of business is related to the structural configuration including primarily important of the decision-making method. A company structure is independently but will not guarantee favorable developments, if they're not the utilizing level of management. Is management obligation, to set up the rational company directions, the proper compliance, the appropriate motivations, the correct individual plus the reasonable success. Once a company experiences productivity, and developments, the company structural design needs to be rearranged.

Company structure design including its core elements will change from company to company, but one thing is common to all thriving businesses. That is the association of the structural design to imperative plans also the demands of the situation.

The Core Elements

The core elements of any company structure transpire fundamentally throughout the creating process, however, may also transpire at the company undergoing of maturity also developments. Also, during the summation of starting your business, the type of structure of the business. Such as Sole Proprietorship, S or C Corporation, LLC, or Limited would facilitate the advantageous performance. Last the core element of the company image, mission statement, goals, and operational business plan.

The core elements must be imagined too with various parts in mind. The circumstances involve recognizing what the obvious intent is for the company. For example, what services, merchandise, the location, and potential projected growth.

After the 2005 Bankruptcy of my company plus learning how to become a transformational leader I ventured out to the state of Massachusetts taking an underwriting job with a Bank. The organization provided banking and mortgage services, Conventional loan, FHA, VA, plus commercial loan. Because of this I became a transformational leader. A transformational leader, "is a style of leadership where the leader is charged with identifying the needed change, willingness and ability to make things personal, to engage others openly, and to spotlight successes as they emerge inspiration and executing the change in tandem with committed members of the group." (Wikimedia Foundation, Inc., a non-profit organization. 2015). At this point in my life, I went from a CEO to a management style. I had to learn to humanize myself in a humility way. Humility means putting everyone, but yourself into a higher value. Making the transformation essential, I learned how hard people have to work for money. How employees are under a salary, plus work over 40 hours for a salary of $45,000 to 60,000 a year.

Transformations command exceptional response: to employees. Obligation essentially in reshaping the company while maintaining a good management style. At the bank, I had to find where my energy came from on each day to day with the customer. You had rich or poor customers, super credit or bad credit customer that came into the back. A powerful transformation account at the bank was helping workers believe a purpose by acknowledging them. I also notice with the range of how I was helping, it achieves an emotional status at the office. The transformation changed the company down to how accommodate loan for the customer. The ultimate impact gave me a promotion to Sr. underwriting after one year with the company. The reward was simple listen to customer, call them back, plus send a birthday card. That was the system I impose that earn me a reward of raise to Sr. Underwriter.

However, as the company expands, I recognize that it was becoming too challenging to stay on the front of the decision-making. Also, realizing my salary was just a portion of what I used to make as a CEO. I decided to call it quits at the end of 2007 to move back home to create another business.

Conceptual Transformation

After I had departed from the bank, I believed that I had evolved to be a conceptual Leader. The Jobs enabled me to be an administrator and to envision the entire business plus work with ideas and the relationships within difficult thoughts.

A conceptual leader defines as "Favorites the ability to think creatively about, analyze and understand complicated and abstract ideas. Using a well-developed conceptual skill set, Top level business managers need to be able to look at their company as a holistic entity, to see the interrelationships between its divisions, and to understand how the firm fits into and affects its overall environment."(Business Dictionary. 2015).

Conclusion

Overall this is how I evolved in 20 years to become a conceptual management philosopher, with principles, values, and a style that best describes me as an individual. At the end of 2007 I started another business into Government contracting, today the business still stand profitable. I have come full circle of the conceptual leader from both sides of the aisle. At the end of 2013 I embark on achieving a doctoral degree in business management. As my understanding developed throughout my education, I have been able to reminisce of the paragon of learner ship that goes with the business hand on hand. All company enterprise is reliant upon the respective determination. Is the determination have made as my company CEO to accomplished my Ph.D. The conception of a company, the purpose of the construction, the interior including external circumstances, decision-making style, communication style, including the leadership are all a combination of teamwork.

An evolving leadership is a better leader, a better judgment of an individual. A decision-making style that is based on "skill set, top level business managers need to be able to look at their company as a holistic entity."(Business Dictionary., 2015).

References

Business Dictionary. (2015).

http://www.businessdictionary.com/definition/conceptual-skill.html.

Wikimedia Foundation, Inc., (2015). A non-profit organization.tps://en.wikipedia.org/wiki/Transformational_leadership.

Printed in the United States
By Bookmasters